MIXED COMPANY

Phoenix·Poets

A SERIES EDITED BY ALAN SHAPIRO

ALAN SHAPIRO

Mixed company

To Ted & Virginia
with great affection
Alan   2/6/96

THE UNIVERSITY OF CHICAGO PRESS
Chicago & London

Alan Shapiro is professor of English and creative writing at the University of North Carolina, Chapel Hill. He is the author of four previous books of poetry, including *Happy Hour* (1987), which was awarded the William Carlos Williams Award by the Poetry Society of America, and most recently of *Covenant* (1991). He is also the author of a collection of essays entitled *In Praise of the Impure: Poetry and the Ethical Imagination* (1993).

The University of Chicago Press, Chicago 60637
The University of Chicago Press, Ltd., London
© 1996 by The University of Chicago
All rights reserved. Published 1996
Printed in the United States of America

05 04 03 02 01 00 99 98 97 96   1 2 3 4 5

ISBN 0–226–75030–2 (cloth)
      0–226–75031–0 (paper)

Library of Congress Cataloging-In-Publication Data

Shapiro, Alan, 1952–
      Mixed company/ Alan Shapiro.
          p. cm. — (Phoenix poets)
      I. Title. II. Series.
      PS3569.H338M58   1996
      811'.54—dc20   95-35099
                                                              CIP

This book is for my son and daughter, Nat and Isabel

Contents

Acknowledgments

The author wishes to thank the following magazines and journals in which these poems or versions of them first appeared:

Atlantic Monthly: "Night Terrors"
Boston Review: "In the Land of the Inheritance"
DoubleTake: "Black Maid," "The Fight," and "Between Assassinations"
The Paris Review: "Pleasure"
Poetry: "Sisters," and "Soul"
The Threepenny Review: "The Letter," and "Ex-Wife: Infatuation"
TriQuarterly: "Mother: Sun Bathing," "Single Mother," "Lethe," "Woman Friend," "Manufacturing," and "The Basement"
Western Humanities Review: "My Mother and a Few Friends"

"The Letter" was selected for inclusion in the anthology *Best American Poetry 1994,* edited by A. R. Ammons. "Manufacturing" was selected for inclusion in the anthology *Best American Poetry 1995*, edited by Richard Howard.

The author also thanks the Lila Wallace–Reader's Digest Fund for a Lila Wallace–Reader's Digest Writer's Award, and the National Endowment for the Arts for a fellowship in poetry, both of which greatly aided in the writing of these poems.

The Letter

The letter said you had to speak to me.
Please, if you love me, Alan, hurry. Please.

I read it and reread it, running down
the big stone steps into the underground,

and every time, as in an anagram,
the letters rearranged themselves again

as new words canceling the ones before:
Come or don't come I really couldn't care . . .

I never meant to hurt you like I did . . .
I never hurt you. There's nothing to forgive . . .

The letter virulent with changing moods,
now cross, now pleading, accusing and accused,

seemed to infect each place I hurried through:
the slippery concrete of the vestibule,

the long low tunnel, and the turnstiles where
nobody waited to collect my fare,

nobody on the platform either, far
and near no sound within that mineral air,

nothing around me but a fever of clues
of what it was you wanted me to do.

O mother, my Eurydice in reverse,
was it the white line I was meant to cross?

To hear within its Thou Shalt Not a "Shall"
and follow you into a lower hell?

The page went blank. Below me now I saw
barbed wire running where the third rail was,

and in the sharp script of its angry weaving,
suspended in the loops and snares, the playthings

of forgotten life, dismembered dolls,
the frayed tip of a rubber knife, a wheel,

the tiny shatterings of cups and saucers,
and other things worn back into mere matter,

their glitter indecipherable except
as the star burst of some brief interest,

the barbed discarded relics of a wanting
they all intensified by disappointing.

As if they could be words, and those words yours,
obscuring what they substituted for,

each leading to a darker one beyond
the bleak lights of the platform, I jumped down

and there at last among them crawled and read,
burning with comprehension as I bled.

The pain was good, the pain exhilarated,
the pain was understanding, now perfected.

Cauled in my own blood, mute and lame and free
of everything obstructing you from me,

I saw your face above me leaning down.
There's nothing here for you, you said, *go home.*

It's for your own good, child, believe me, and
I vanished, waking as you turned around.

My Mother and a Few Friends

My mother and a few friends at a table,
talking, smoking, entirely at ease
because alone at last. I'm somewhere there
among them, but too small to matter, made
invisible, it seems, by everything
I don't yet know. The men are gone, as usual,
where I couldn't say for certain, though
it's easy to imagine them as having
drifted away together, groggy with eating,
to go on talking money, money, meaning
who got taken for a fucking, and by whom,
and for how much. But now, if heard at all,
their voices reach us from so faraway
that nothing of what they say's discernible
beyond the half-consoling, half-dyspeptic
rhythm of the adages they answer
one another with—"Business is business" . . . "You got
to speculate if you want to accumulate . . ."
"The only thing that grows in your hand is your pecker. . ."

Who else beside my mother's at the table?
B.Z., Pearl, Gissy, Dot, or Ann?
And anyway to know this and be able
then to say with confidence they're close
to the beginning of more than forty years
of just such afternoons, before this one

dies, or that one moves away, or sickens,
is not to make it any easier
to look beyond my having known them now
for so long otherwise, as middle-aged,
as old, and see them as I saw them then.

Even my mother's vague, being so young,
her face so much a restless shadowy
idea of being young, and stylish:
the blonde hair tinted blonder, teased and sprayed,
the just-so hint of rouge, the glistening lips,
her features (like the features of her friends)
meticulously shaped to the desire
for the thoroughly prescribed, thoroughly
extraordinary future all her own.

By then, of course, enough of their real future
(though only enough perhaps) would have arrived
to make that general postwar thrilled
expectancy as difficult to be
believed in as abandoned. By then, too,
even among each other, there would have been
the usual envies, petty grievances,
slights and disappointments. I know, I know.
And yet despite this (even perhaps because
of this as well), the picture of them there,
and of myself among them, is a picture
somehow haunted still by happiness:
happiness too peculiar to themselves, though,
too elusive being so much theirs,
so near, so ordinary.

                The women keep
on talking, and I watch and watch, and all
I make out clearly is the cigarette

now one and now another hand is waving
into strands of smoke that tangle and run
together whenever anybody speaks;
I watch until it seems the voices are
themselves that swirling gauze, secretive, communal,
hung there to say, whatever else the words
were saying, we are this, and they are that.

Mother: Sun Bathing

While you're at it, do my legs too,
and your friend rose from the chaise
beside yours, tucking and jiggling
the unstrapped black bathing suit
still farther up over her heavy bust
so she could lean down safely, spread
the white cream across your back,
your shoulders, kneading it gently
down all over you until your skin
shone in the drowsy wake
of where her hands were drifting.

You were younger than I am now,
and I was how old, five? six?
dawdling near you though you had
told me to go play already,
dawdling just far enough away
to see you through the eddying
of waists and knees, flipflops,
hips and hands, to hear your voice
among the surf of voices, made strange
now by that other woman's hands:

your voice no longer skewed, divided,
craving what it said it had—
the "stunning" husband, the "such wonderful" kids,

the too radiant dream the words made
from which the tone was always waking,
angry in praise, bitter in pleasure,
there and not there; to make my listening,
even when spoken to, an overhearing
of an argument I wasn't meant
to follow, my anxious legacy.

Now, though, you spoke grunts, mewlings,
frank creaturely oohs in answer
to the hands that slid down one
and then another leg and calf
and went on rubbing long after
there was nothing left to rub.

Now listening, too, was so much
having that I could move back
up the beach to where your voice
was only half yours, half the water's,
then entirely the water's,
and I could now step toward you
and believe the glittering wide
belly of the sea itself
was pleasure, and that your voice rose
only out of pleasure to my ear.

Widows

They may as well be talking to themselves,
my great-aunts Ann and Tilly, except they need
to hear each other's story to believe
their own is listened to, their conversation
a separate yet companionable dreaming
on the front porch of the badly weathered beach house
Ann and her husband bought back in the forties.
First summer here, Ann says, without my Burt.
And Tilly answers, Jack, my Jack,—you know,
it's twenty years he's gone last Christmas,
remember when he did the wiring
for Hershner's Candy, how he'd bring me home
a bag of chocolate every day, such chocolate,
oh, you could die it was so delicious, he
was such a gentleman. And Ann says, yes,
my Burt, he was a prince, so wonderful,
he was always so wonderful to me, to the kids . . .

All afternoon, the family blurs about them,
grandchildren and great-grandchildren, nephews, nieces,
going and coming between the house and water,
the water that from here is neither seen
nor heard but felt mostly as an incredibly
distant tremor in the porch's floor.
All afternoon, they happily ignore us,
wholly absorbed within the separate pleasures

of remembering what they remember,
forgetting what they forget, as if to talk
this way about their lives were the reward
itself for having gotten life behind them.

It is as if their conversation were
a sea they turn about on freely, each
in her own craft, side by side: unmoored from fact,
unfettered by their accumulated losses,—
turn freely about to see the shore behind them,
the sturdy muddle of their marriages
now far enough away to be the marriages
they should have had, that they deserved.
Beyond the screen of surf they look through now
they find their husbands, tiny and indistinct:
the prince who was so wonderful to her,
the gentleman who used to bring her chocolate.

Matriarchs

No afterworld for them.
At the threshold of it
the estranging thrill

of having nothing
anymore to mother
will make them

have to turn back here
among us by the water
where we bring our children—

to believe that vigilant stern
cosseting against what happens
anyway is really over.

Heaven for them will be
a clinging to the fierce
exertion they once were—

so they can now feel
only their freedom
from it; heaven

for them will be
the perpetual surprise
of being pleased

our voices, calling
to the children not
to wander off too far

into the water,
thin away
to kelp rot,

brine, to mere
hallucinations
of the air's immeasurable

tide of old dispersals;
Heaven, for them,
will be the knowledge

that their lives were spent
resisting what their bodies,
even then, were given

over to each moment,
that the cauled head
crowning at the bloody

edge was the beginning
of what now will carry them,
with all time, sooner or later,

back into the very rooms
they tended, to settle there
as haze, as yellowings,

over the surfaces they
never could get clean
enough. Here is their heaven,

here where they are what
they had to clean away,
what they would warn against

among the tangling
boom of water,
wraiths of salt spray,

and extravagant space
we have to hurl our voices
over till our children hear.

Wife: Labor

The pain inhaled you,
and you groaned it out in no voice
I had ever heard before, a voice
anterior to yours, archaic, fierce,
from so far deep within you
I could hear the rock vein, mineral
mother-lode
the aboriginal
first freak of pulse was
ripped from
once and now returned to
for the force it needed.
And as the head crowned,
as the blood-crowned
head emerged it was
your body only now that spoke,
your face unrecognizable,
wrenched tight as rope,
hands twisting in the sheets,
and what it started to
say then in anguish,
blood, excrement, it
finished saying later
when the nipple
between your fingers brushed
the baby's cheek so deftly
that she turned to suck:

you would have died to save her
if you had to, and if she died
you would have raged,
you would have grieved and lived.

Isabel

When you were three days old, your mother sang to you.
Cradling you at last, holding to your mouth the tube
of oxygen you couldn't breathe without, for the first time
in a voice made tentative with gladness still too new to trust,
more brave than beautiful, she sang your name, sang
over you the quavering song of every syllable she wanted
to prolong, to keep repeating till she was certain
the astonished welcome of it had settled in your ear
so deeply that you would hear her singing even later
when the singing stopped and you were taken from her.

Despite the panting lungs, the bruised arms, the tubes and wires,
how calm you seemed then (even the doctor noticed),
Watching you both, I knew as I've known little else
that years from now, alone, in company, waking
or edging into sleep, when over you there falls
as if from nowhere, too suddenly to be explained,
a joyous sense of being wanted here in the world,—

not knowing that you are, you'll be remembering this.

Night Terrors

Whose voice is it in mine when the child cries,
terrified in sleep, and half asleep myself I'm there
beside him saying, shh, now easy, shh,

whose voice—too intimate with all the ways
of solace to be merely mine; so prodigal
in desiring to give, yet so exact in giving

that even before I reach the little bed,
before I touch him, as I do anyway,
already he is breathing quietly again.

Is it my mother's voice in mine, the memory
no memory at all but just the vocal trace,
sheer bodily sensation on the lips and tongue,

of what I may have heard once in the pre-
remembering of infancy—heard once and then
forgot entirely till it was wakened by the cry,

brought back, as if from exile, by the child's cry,—
here to the father's voice, where the son again
can ask the mother, and the mother, too, the son—

Why has it taken you so long to come?

Hecuba

for Martha Nussbaum

All night, sirens near
and far and never
quite out of hearing
trouble the child's sleep.

He cries, help, help, dogs
chasing me, his voice
too porous with dream
now, and dream with world,

to let the cries stop
till my arms have brought
around him the re-
assurance nothing

bad can happen here.
For hours the sirens
seem to hound him in
and out of thin sleep,

though I hold him, sing
to him a little,

learning again my
helplessness through his,

and through mine, sensing
yours now, Queen mother,
hopeless nurturer;—
my dread, the faintest

inkling of the bleak
clarity of your
unspeakable end
when you discover

once and for all what
you knew anyway,
that the maternal
voice too is a plant,

a green shoot fragile
as the flesh it bore
and worried over
day and night: voice like

the dear flesh of your
hundred children—fed
so reliably
from the ancestral

soil of vow and law
and customary
bond it didn't need
even to notice

it was being fed
at all till the food

was spoiled, the ancient
city burned, razed, all

in a moment made
a necropolis
of children, and speech,
too, the mother tongue,

nothing but a mere
husk flimsy as ash
the voice was stripped of
to its howling core.

Only sirens here
disturb my child's sleep,
tracing a random
havoc that isn't

likely to touch him,
not here at least, not
tonight. Nonetheless,
it's you I think of

as I hold him, rock
him, as you rocked yours,
alert as you were,
though it did no good,

singing as you did
in a voice that love,
to be love, must keep
doggedly singing,

keep tenuous and
fierce because it knows

the world is always
here and everywhere,

even in the song
the voice sings, even
in the sleep it brings,
now only worldless

enough to let him
be, if nothing else,
ready to waken
when he has to wake.

Single Mother

1.

I can recognize the tiny subterfuge: how the mother,
giving her child exactly what he's asked for, has escaped him
without him knowing that she has: higher, he said, higher,
until she hardly has to push the swing now and can
safely close her eyes, and doze, and for a moment
        not be anybody's mother.

The price of that leisure, though, is to be startled
when he cries, to feel ashamed, too, by the sweetness
the cry disperses. So that she seems almost to wish
her voice, full of more solace than he cries for now,
could deepen his distress and so intensify for him
        the pleasure of her taking it away.

2.

Most mornings he's up at five, she says. By nine, bored, cranky,
he wants to go somewhere but won't let her dress him, wants to eat
but not anything she offers. Then he starts crying for daddy, he wants
his daddy. That's when the weariness turns suddenly to rage,
her body one white knuckle of rage, and she has to get him quick
out of the house, somewhere where just the presence of another
mother will protect them both from what she otherwise might do.

3.

His first and last assumption. His given,
as enveloping as air, and like air
to his breathing, unrecognized

as needed, being always there.
Moody weather he wakes up to,
atmosphere perpetually charged

with emerging and dispersing
fronts and pressures that are themselves
the indecipherable effects

of earlier weather in another sky
he can't see yet is helpless
not to read for any omen of himself.

Beyond which only the outer space
of not her goes on and on.
Everywhere beyond her what

her distractions, daydreams, brief
luxuries of blank attention
hint at, and make him have to cry

sometimes to call her back from;
what his dark bedroom hints at
when she leaves it, too tired

not to, though he calls and cries,
too obviously glad, yes glad
for a short while at least,

to leave him finally in the nowhere
of her hurrying away,
fleeing momentarily away

for once to where no gravity
at all can keep her from forgetting
her relief can only mean his terror.

4.

The moment my son and I arrived she started talking,
at swing first, then at sandbox, while the boys played,

talking incessantly in a low drawl of exhaustion
one could easily mistake for a drugged calm.

As if her voice just couldn't wake, it seemed to sleepwalk
through a single sentence, incontinent with revelation,

about how they have no choice now but to put up
living with her mother till she can find a job,

because her ex-husband, among other things,
couldn't stand the mess the boy made when he ate,

and how his tantrums scare her, he can really lose it,
especially in public, which is so humiliating,

what are you supposed to do in front of all those people?
and does mine love Bambi as much as hers?

and did I ever notice that the mother's always killed off
in those movies, or locked up, or somehow gotten

out of the way before the child does anything
at all remarkable to show he's worthy

of growing up into a prince, or star, or daddy? . . .
Despite the drab sweatsuit, the squall of unkempt hair,

the deep fatigue around the eyes and mouth, there was
about her a stubborn loveliness I can't pretend

I didn't notice whenever she would, yawning, arch
her torso toward me just a little, or when her long hands

seemed to parry, in slow arabesques and curliques,
the thrusts of what she couldn't help herself from saying.

Wouldn't it be less than honest not to say I listened,
or appeared to listen, not out of sympathy alone?

that listening was the coin I paid to take her in
more freely, to revel in my own way in the little

resonance of possibility our being there
with children made it completely safe for me to feel?

And if she suspected this and went on talking
to me anyway, as if I were the dreamed-of mother

or friend whose ear she always had the pleasure of,—
so desperate to be listened to, to be coddled with listening,

that she'd indulge my eye, so she could have herself
this ersatz intimacy,—wasn't it, all in all, a fair transaction?

Not children anymore, don't we at times use each other,
pay each other one way or another for the pleasures

that, however briefly, bring us to the child's
exhilaration that the mother can't not hear or come?

The way she heard when the boy called and immediately
hurried over to see what it was he wanted.

And the way, too, suddenly like a girl, she swung herself
as if no weight restrained her onto the monkey bar,

to hang there upside down above him, laughing,
swinging, holding her hands out so her fingertips

would graze his when he leaped up to grab her,
leaped and missed. And even though he started to cry,

though he was crying now, she howled like a monkey
for a moment longer, just for the pleasure of it.

5.

The night-light diffuses paler darkness through the dark
around him, soothing for now, from his features, all fevers

of appetite; all spasms of raw will ease,
effaced in such excess of peace there's little

left of him but dream sounds, mews, sighs, vexing
the silence so faintly they seem to deepen it.

Here, at least, is patience, inexhaustible
so long as there's nothing else to worry over

but the covers she has to put back gently again,
and again, across him when he turns or shifts.

Here now his breathing is the tide she drifts on
toward sleep at last, but slowly, not yielding yet,

though sleep is all she's yearned for all day long.
She holds it off, delays it, to prolong

this present moment of a mothering
that isn't withering her, or marring him.

Sylvia

I.

All he needed was a dog, you said,
in that last conversation on the street
just weeks before you killed yourself. A dog,
didn't I think, would keep him out of trouble
till you got home? Not that he'd been in any
really, no more than any boy his age.
Your voice too edgy in its cheery lilt
to be believed, breathless with schemes, solutions,
lessons that never came to anything
but seemed to soften the hard luck enough
for you to tell about it, time and again,
in every conversation, your first child's death
ten years ago, how you can thank god for it now,
it's taught you to be such a better mother,
and how your drunken ex just hangs around
and hangs around, though you put up with it
for the boy's sake, so he can see up close
the kind of man he shouldn't ever be . . .

You were so tedious to listen to.
I wonder if you knew it, and knowing it
were no less helpless to do anything
to stop it. And if there wasn't something else
I should have heard that last time in your voice
(although to hear it would have made no difference),

something my pity, maybe, and impatience,
prevented me from hearing,—some last flare
of remorseless dignity compelling you
to say as always, even then, I'm fine,
I'm handling everything, when what you meant
was look how terribly I've had to suffer.

You must have seen that last time how I shifted,
how frankly by then I glanced away, blamed you
for having left me no polite way out.
For you just smiled as I abruptly turned,
smiled and said again, it almost seemed
as much for my sake now as yours, no need
to worry, really, a dog would do the trick.

2.

If it only took a moment to decide,
if out of all you suffered there had been
one moment in particular that made

the choice seem good, that drew you to the notion
that that last inscription in the Book of Life
would unredeemably obliterate

whatever else was written on your page;
if only a single moment could have clinched it,
likely as not, could this have been the one:

caught in my headlights on the steep curve of the street:
the dog was loose again, and you just home
from work, in high heels stumbling after him,

the leash swinging from one hand like a scourge
against your hip, knee, shin whenever you faltered,
and your face taut, holding back expression, brightly

expressing nothing, saying this is nothing,
no need to stop the car, it's just another
little thing is all, no big deal, no problem,

till the lights released you, and you hurried on
unsteadily for an instant in the rear view,
then beyond it as you turned the corner.

Wife: The Good Daughter

That voice of yours, last night,
ill at ease with pleasure,
quavering as it described
how a colleague you were sure
disliked you praised you
in front of others;

that slight upward tremulous
tic, that wood-knocking
inflection of triumph
with apology for triumph,
of "give me" with excuse
for "give me," was it the echo

of the good child you were?—
the child too good to think
her anger at the fanfare
all the others make
over the prodigal's
merest gesture of consideration

(while her own dull daily
offices, because presumed,
go unremarked upon)
means anything but that
she isn't good enough.
Not your only voice, I know,

yet it saddened me
to hear it, to realize
not least of what is
loveliest about you
is just this thwarted wish
that you were otherwise.

Wife: The Mirror

The softest part of his anatomy
was the bristling hint of hair on the shaved head.
The t-shirt tight as spandex on the pecs,
the shoulders, the rippling stomach, seemed to sharpen
the definition of what it covered up.
With a god's composure, or an animal's,
leaning against the lamp post, he was gazing,
nakedly gazing at all the passing women
(even the ones that other men were with),
gazing and smiling a stainless certitude
that they would think it was their privilege
he'd notice them at all.

                     I thought of those
sometimes protracted times when you and I
have been invisible to one another,
distracted, or at odds, and how at such
times often after showering I'll watch myself
and feel, though wishing this were firmer, that
were bigger, not entirely displeased,
imagining another woman sees
the way mist on the mirror makes a kind
of nimbus all around me as it clears.

I thought of other times as well, times when
you come to me in need of comfort only,

only desiring to be held, and I mistake it,
and either push on in a blind assurance
that what I want is really all you need,
or sulk away, to lick the wounded ego.

Suddenly I could see him through your eyes.
I realized the fugitive dislike
you would have showed in face or voice—
had you been there with me—would not have been
for that man only, but for the very thing
he purified of hesitation, doubt.
It would have been dislike for that male gaze,
that ever vigilant aim, that too precise,
impersonal and solitary heat.

Pleasure

Ever obliging, faithful, good parents that they are,
when he's happiest, in his happy bed, his wife against him,
they call to him, his tutelary spirits of a moment
hidden now inside his pleasure, as his pleasure's underground.
They call, and the rapt eclipse, the mutual gasp and cry,
is suddenly the golden bough leading him back down stairs,
a child again, to the doorway where his mother stumbles,
yelling something, with her arms held like a shield before her
as his father swings,—just that, and nothing else beyond it,
no before, no after, and no terror either but the terror
of remembering that he was thrilled, not terrified at all,
as if they knew what would please him before he did himself,
tightening all along the coil of what he didn't know
was there, of what they hid from him so he would feel
only the sheer pleasure of its fierce release.
It was their first, their clearest lesson in fulfillment.
Ever after only the tantalizing substitutes, the sulks
and silences, the spectral pantomimes, that left him
more expectant, hungry, dreaming the ever more vivid
dream of what they wouldn't do, withheld, he realizes now,
so he'd always want that pleasure, know how incomparable it was.
Here, where he's happiest, with his wife beside him, his hand
no heavier than breath along her arm and shoulder, they bring
him back to that original event because they love him, flesh
of their flesh, they want him to have everything they had.

Lethe

You called me to come see the bees. Come out of the house
you called once, in a bad time, when we were lost to each other,
blurred by habitual regard, disgruntled and aloof
though not from injuries, but from a hoarded sense
of being injured, precious so long as vague, vague
        so long as silent.

By the marigolds you planted they were all hovering,
hundreds of bees, it seemed, like bright flecks of the lavish
blossoms they were drawn to, each long stalk tipping over
under the pressure as they clung together, crowded and swarmed
the way Vergil says the souls do by the waters
        in Elysium:

even there among the blessed groves, the lush green
of bodiless pleasure, weightless now, unstrictured,
free, they swarm to drink oblivion and again put on
the body's weight. I leaned down close to look, to see
what you saw, and as I did, unconsciously you rested
        one hand on my shoulder,

in an old way, dormant for how long? Time, unresting time,
beautiful and perverse, how suddenly it could lift us
clear of our own shade to a luminous attention
it just as suddenly extinguished, as the bees moved on,
the shade, now, darker for that brief respite. *Poor souls*, Aeneas asks,
        how can they crave our daylight so?

Ex-Wife: Infatuation

Your voice more bashful the more intimate
it grew on that first night, an indrawn breath
of speech I can't recall beyond the miserly
sweet way it hesitated on the tongue,
chary of giving, chary of taking back,
the same breath doing both at once, it seemed,
to draw me to a closer kind of speech;

yet knowing too, knowing even then
what I—more loved than loving—had the clumsy
luxury not to know, that all too soon
what words we had to say would fail us, each
lingering syllable a syllable less
between the pleasure it held off and invited,

and the bad luck pleasure would become;
a sweet syllable closer to the other nights,
the last nights, nights that would make remembering
that long first night the bitter cost of having
had what we were on the verge of having.

Ex-Wife: Homesickness

Voice that would wake me
in the bland American
too anywhereness
of the rented room we lived in,—
on those last nights
together when realizing
you would soon leave
seemed to revive so
cruelly our earliest delights
in one another;

voice not meant for my ears,
risen, it seemed, from some
never before sounded
privacy within you,
permitting you to hear—
as you murmured that
you wanted to go home
to Ireland, home, home,—
how the word you thought
would speak only your longing

now spoke grief, spoke
dread, and not for me,
or us, or anything
at all you'd leave behind,

but for the very thing
you wanted to go home to,
everything you'd find
before the hearth fire,
drink in hand, sheer
animal solace in the sound

of wind and slant rain
at the gabled window,
against the roof and walls,
the room all lair, all burrow,
and you within it safer
for the storm's familiar
harrowing that kept
your need to be at home
there, always,
not inordinate.

Sisters

for Sheila

Now as helpless either to imagine
       the last edge of awareness
or stop trying to,

as sister love calls you back
       and back to the unbridgeable
moment between her

and her no longer who she was;
       whatever it was she felt,
or knew, or saw,

may it be possible for you now
       at least to think of her free
of anything

that might still hold her to what she has
       to leave and so add only more
affliction to the leaving;

may it be possible, at least,
       to think of her surprised
for once by ease,

by being thoroughly relieved,
       as when a muscle clenched
for so long

makes it difficult to recognize
       the pain as pain—
until it's gone.

Soul

If, as they always claim upon returning,
there's only radiance there, near death, and in
that radiance the brighter densities of all
their own beloved dead come out to greet them,
and they themselves now bodiless, rinsed clean
of eye or ear, are able to perceive them;
if it's the after-image of the body
only, the thinning yet still sentient mist
of who they were, that keeps them only far
enough away from what they brighten toward
to know themselves as its auroral edge;—
Why then do they return?

                Couldn't it instead
be the body that rejoices there?
that radiance the body's radiance
of being only just aware enough
as body to know it is itself the star-
flung anonymity it's on the verge of
when the suddenly too quiet quiet
startles the soul awake, and soul comes rushing,
calling and rushing like a fearful and
ferocious mother to her only child?

Lover

Since we can greet and be greeted only
        through the separate
and not entirely intelligible

languages of "membrane, joynt or limb,"
        and therefore
must with every greeting yearn

more urgently for the angelic
        congress
we are barred from forever—

spirits intermixing "easier
        than air with air";
since it is only distance here

that joins us in the misaligned
        or unequal
effort we exert to overcome it,

and all distance, even the smallest,
        even when we seem
to touch, to understand each other,

is a desert, what can we finally do
        but love the desert,
love the shimmering air

of one another that recedes
        as we approach it,
love most of all the approach,

the heat, the thirst that can make
        of our ever
meeting here together,

in any way at all,
        a virtual,
if not miraculous, water.

Girlfriend

The perfect match:
both of us sixteen
and showing it:
I in my rush
to do what I had
never done before,
and you in yours
to prove you had:
each other's bit and spur,
your shaky know-how
made convincing
by my ignorance;
my fumbling hand
requiring, even
grateful for the voice
more school marm
than madam, that made sure
as it led me so
fastidiously on,
over and into
each willing part of you
that there'd be no
at any point mistaking
your bidding
for my liberty.

You'd be, of course,
a better judge of this
than I, but I now think
I was the kind of student
eager to answer
correctly
everything he's asked
in order not to please
the teacher so much as
to avoid all the attention
being wrong can bring.
In other words, trying
hard to follow
everywhere you led
was really just for me
a way of being left
alone, however happily,
with all the pleasure
pleasing you
(or thinking anyway I had)
enabled me to take.

There was hardly any break
then when it was over.
And it even seemed
you excused yourself
so I could picture
all of it more freely
to myself, in unencumbered
solitude, devising,
rearranging, slowing
down and dwelling
studiously on
what we had rushed through
and was merely foreplay
now to what perfected it.

It was then I heard you
in the next room on the phone,
that giggling whisper to your friend,
that girlish tune
of scorn that told me
without your knowing
that it did, that you were there,
that I was not alone.
Oh, it has dogged me
down the years, that voice,
reliable as conscience,
and as sharp,
whenever I assume
now things are well
since I am well;
whenever I grow too free
in pleasure, too certain,
brash, that cutting
giggle from another room
reminds me, not so fast.

Woman Friend

What is the place of friendship between a man
and woman when they deny, for friendship's sake,
whatever may have drawn them first together
and still draws them now even more avidly
      for having been resisted?

What kind of place, when each seems to the other
everything their marriages no longer give,
or never did; the two of them unable
not to be each other's sly dream of a life
      impervious to time,

born of the very limits it will not heed?
How haunted are their settled intimacies;
the known lip or hand, the most familiar touch,
pleasure less keen than comfortable, now made new
      in their estrangement from it.

How odd, too, to be nearly lovers, freest
with each other only in their spouse's arms,
passionate when the passion is imagined,
and, therefore, at their most passionate, to be
      most sumptuously withdrawn.

See how such friendship makes unnatural
anywhere they find themselves together,
like snow that freezes only at the least hint
of thaw, any sign at all of muffled heat.
     See how the very air

between them makes a windchill of desire—
the more they try to say to one another,
the colder grows the air; the air grows colder,
emptier, precisely for the way the words
     steam, and the steam vanishes.

The Friend

Figdeting with the beer she doesn't drink,
one finger picking at the softening label,
careful to peel one corner, then the other
free, without it tearing, she tells me
she much prefers pain to embarrassment,
and everything about the whole affair—
that Karl had been both her and her husband's oldest,
closest friend, that they had coddled him
through two failed marriages, and when their own
faltered, that he'd become her confidant,
and then, of course, her lover—everything now
but his betrayal's so degradingly
predictable in a suburban pot-
boiler sort of way that the betrayal
itself seems almost redemptive, almost a gift.

Joe never suspected anything, too busy
making up excuses for the book
he couldn't get around to writing—he needed
better software, the apartment was too noisy,
her presence distracted him too much, her absence
put too much pressure on him to produce . . .
just once in all those years of working, putting
her own ambitions off so he could bask
fretfully in the glow of his potential,
just once she would have liked to say, please, darling,

take all your clothes off, stand before the mirror,
and ask yourself, for once, now really, does this
look like the center of the universe?

And yet it took those long first intimate talks
with Karl to realize just how lonely she'd
become, how angry, how dissatisfied.
Yet less for anything he might have said
than for the way he simply listened to her,
he had a woman's way of listening,
sympathetic, compassionate, engrossed,
with none of that distrustful, briney-with-judgment
air of insecurity she'd grown
accustomed to. And it was woman-like,
as well, the way he utterly forgave
his ex-wives for their flaws, mistakes, deceptions,
yet seemed so merciless about his own;
the way he showed such deft, exquisite feeling
for the messily extenuating, nearly
indecipherable relatedness
of how things happen, so that the more he told,
the more she in response would tell until
she found herself confiding things she thought
she'd never ever say to anyone.

By then, going to bed had come to seem
merely the next inevitable step
to a yet deeper conversation. Well,

o.k., she was a fool not to have seen
where that one led. She should have known Karl,
being a man, like any man, once she
was free, would hem and haw the feeblest things,
straight from the Soaps, about him needing time,
he's so confused, he cares so much about her . . .

and on and on until you didn't need
a psychic to foretell the clichés those clichés
were leading to: cold feet, cold shower, cold storage.

If that were all, though, she could write him off
as a delusion born of the disease
her marriage was, humiliating, yes,
and sad too, yet not really that disastrous.
Even the sex, though good, was mostly just
the novelty of being wanted once again.
Why she might even feel now that she should thank him
for having helped her get out of the marriage.
If that were all. If not for the betrayal.

No, the betrayal changed him, made him, she
admits, more interesting because more vexing.
Or maybe it's the other way around.
In any event, the puzzle of it isn't
that he and Joe throughout the whole affair
would often get together behind her back
(so Joe would tell her later, to punish her
when he found out what they had done to him),
or that they met here at this bar, at this
particular table where she and Karl would go
to talk, where she and I talk now. Or that
Karl was the one who would arrange the meetings,
who'd try to draw Joe out. Or even that
the two of them discussed her. No, it was
what he would tell Joe when Joe began to fear
that he was losing her: night in, night out,
sometimes before he'd see her, sometimes
afterward, from this table to her bed,
from her bed to this table, he would go
to Joe and tell him, Joe, don't be a fool,
whatever you have to do to keep her, do.

And looking down now at her hands, as if
they're hardly hers as they begin to shred
the label into small and smaller pieces,
she wants to know if I was aware of this,
since Karl was my friend too, and still is?
And I say, no, not really. Which is true,
I wasn't, not of that, at any rate,
although I thought that I knew everything
there was to know about the two of them.
And suddenly now it shames me to remember
my pleasure in those intimate conversations,
how it delighted me to hear Karl say
there's no one else whom I can tell this to
but you. Delighted me he needed my
approval, my acceptance. I realize
I'd have forgiven him almost anything,
even this betrayal, and almost feel
betrayed as well that he would keep it from me.

So for a moment I'm not sure who she means
when she asks, mostly to herself, it seems,—
more troubled than enraged, more curious
than troubled, even cool in the obses-
siveness of the pursuit of what eludes her—
could anyone's attentions be so absorbed,
so voluptuously taken by the moment,
that he himself believes the only friend
he's ever really had is the one he happens
at any given moment to be with?
A friendship junkie? I ask, half-joking,
and she says yes, now looking straight at me,
a friendship junkie, hooked on the sensation
of being thought the perfect friend, the thrill,
too, maybe keener for the coming crash,
the crazy uncontrollable momentum

carrying him along toward certain trouble,
happily not knowing when or where or how.

Or maybe she's got it all wrong, and as she says so
sweeps the tiny pieces off the table.
Maybe he was only all along
so in control that he could make detachment
look and feel like love, like sympathy;
maybe everything, right from the start,
even years ago when she and Joe
were adequately married, if not happily so,
maybe everything even then had been
methodically foreseen, arranged and plotted,—
if that's the case, then was the thrill he sought
the thrill of knowing she believed she'd found
in him the perfect friend, the perfect lover,
while all he'd ever found in her was just
the best available ingredient
for another story that had nothing
at all to do with her, so he could bring
that story where? to what? these very questions
she's unable now to answer or not ask?

She shrugs, and smiles, says all right, now you talk:
what do you think he wanted? And as if
she knew already whatever I might say
but only asked so she could hear me say it,
she's looking past me, bored, when I part guess
and part confess that what he might have wanted,
what might have thrilled him most of all, would be
to know somehow she'd come back here with me,
to talk to me all night about him, talk
all night about him to another friend,
another man who, since he is a man,
must have his own designs upon her. Wouldn't

that be the ultimate kick, I ask, to know this?
But she says nothing, holding her bottle up,
waving it to catch the waiter's eye.
She hasn't listened to a word I've said.

In the Land of the Inheritance

*In those days there was no king in Israel; every man
did what was right in his own eyes.*
                                    —Judges 19–21

A foreigner and his ass and concubine
were huddling in the square as night came on;

around them, veil on veil of dust that hoof
and staff and sandal could only disturb enough

to show how calmly it was sifting down
into a darkening sabbath of its own.

Surely here, he thought, among the Benjamites
someone would ask him in to spend the night,

and he, a holy man, the lord's anointed,
chosen among the chosen. But while he waited,

merchants and tradesmen, young and old alike,
all hurried by without a word or look

to their own dwellings as if he wasn't there,
and only the ache from having come so far,

his sharpening hunger and the night's chill
told him he was not invisible.

His concubine kept silent, her veiled head bowed,
since it was her fault they were stranded now:

Hadn't she tried to run away from him
back to her father's house in Bethlehem,

and when he came to get her, her father said,
"My son, my son," and gave him wine and bread,

and blessed him, and then told the girl, "Go home."
So now he glowered at her. "See what you've done,

impious woman, see what your unclean ways
have brought us to," he was about to say

when an old man who pitied their distress
said, "Peace be to you, friend, come to my house,

I'll give you food for hunger, wine for thirst.
Come to my house, I'll care for all your wants."

Now as they ate and drank, as their hearts grew merry,
the townsmen gathered together in a fury

outside the old man's house and beat his door,
and yelled, "Old man, give us the sojourner

that we may know him, give him to us now."
The old man pleaded, "Leave the man alone,

my brethren, he is a holy man, a priest,
all he has asked for is a place to rest.

Here is my virgin daughter, here is his wife,
take them instead and do what to your sight

seems good to you, but do no wickedness
against the Levite whom the Lord has blessed."

But now like locusts ravaging a field
the men surged forward, shouting, and would not yield

until the Levite, knowing what he owed
the hospitality his host bestowed,

pushed out his wife alone and shut the door.
One by one all night they ravished her.

She ate dirt all night, and when they were through
they left her in a befouling solitude

of being known to each and every man,
exposed and filthy, utterly smeared with sin.

And he, whatever struggle he endured,
hearing her call him at the door he barred,

whatever turbulence of rage and shame
swept through his heart as she called out his name

before the other voices carried hers away,
subsided now as he began to pray,

grew faint, and fainter, until he realized
the Lord was with him, and the Lord was wise.

So even when he discovered her at dawn,
and she just lay there, though he told her, "Come,

let us be going," he knew it had to be
the Lord who guided this iniquity,

who in His marvelous power understood
everything that had happened (and now would),

who steeled within him such a righteous calm
as he laid her on his ass and brought her home—

the Lord's hand holding his that held the knife
and sharpened it and took it to his wife,

and delicately with a jeweler's care
severed limb from joint, and joint from ligature.

All day he worked, he drew the blade down deeper
into the far recess of every chamber

as if each membrane were another veil
he'd cast aside and find the soul revealed.

The soul, however, above the gaping flesh
was hovering, now free of all distress,

serene because she saw what he was doing,
could see as fact the aim he was pursuing—

how all of her, obedient to his will,
would go throughout the land of Israel,

a piece to every tribe, which they'd receive
and be astonished at what it could mean,—

could see them all from Beersheba to Dan
come to the Lord at Mizpah as one man,

four hundred thousand strong, and all now ask
how this abomination came to pass,—

could see them raise their swords together high,
vowing the men of Gibeah would have to die.

So rapt in the unskeining of her vision
of every consequence of his decision,

she almost didn't hear the Lord call, "Come
my Daughter, it's time to come to me, come home."

But she refused, and as his "Daughter, Daughter,"
closed in now echoing everywhere about her,

she let go and dissolved and all He found
was mute dust sifting to the bloody ground,

back to the flesh her husband would disperse
throughout the land of his inheritance.

Manufacturing

Up in the billboard, over old South Station,
the Captain, all wide grin and ruddy cheek,
held up a golden shot of Cutty Sark
high as the skyline where the sunset spread
a gold fan from the twig-like spars and rigging
of a departing clipper ship. Above
the picture the dull haze of a real sun rose,
dragging the day up with it. Seven o'clock.
The agitated horns, brakes, fingers, and catcalls
down below me were already merging
and channeling everybody on to warehouse,
factory, department store and office.

My father and uncle talking over all the goods
to be received that day, the goods delivered,
their two reflections in the window floating
like blurry ghosts within the Captain's grin,
their voices raised a little above the soft
erratic humming of the big machines,
the riveters and pressers, warming, rousing:
The Century order, did it get out last night?
And had the buckles come from Personal?
Who'd go do Jaffey? Who'd diddle Abramowitz
and Saperstein? Those cocksucking sons of bitches,
cut their balls off if they fuck with us . . .

How automatically at any provocation
I can aim the words at anybody now,
woman or man, the reverberating
angry this, not that, in "pussy," "cocksucker,"
"fuckhead," hammered down so far inside me
it's almost too securely there to feel.
But I was thirteen then, and for the first
time old enough to have my father say
these things in front of me, which must have meant
I was a man now too, I listened (blushing,
ashamed of blushing) for clues of what it was
I had become, or was supposed to be:

It did and didn't have to do with bodies,
being a man, it wasn't fixed in bodies,
but somehow passed between them, going to
by being taken from, ever departing,
ever arriving, unstoppable as money,
and moving in a limited supply
it seemed to follow where the money went.
Being a man was something that you did
to other men, which meant a woman was
what other men became when you would do them.
Either you gave a fucking, or you took one,
did or were done to, it was simple as that.

Somebody shouted from beyond the office
that Tony had passed out in the can again.
"The lush, the no good lush," my uncle said,
"get him the fuck out of here for good, will ya."
The stall door swung back, scrawled with giant cocks,
tits, asses and cunts, beyond which in the shadows
my father was gently wrestling with the man,
trying to hold him steady while his free hand
shimmied the tangled shorts and trousers up

over the knees and hips, and even got
the shirt tucked in, the pants zipped deftly enough
for Tony not to notice, though he did.

Even then I knew they'd fire him,
and that it wasn't gratitude at all
that made the man weep inconsolably,
his head bowed, nodding, as my father led him
to the elevator, still with his arm around him,
patting his shoulder, easing him through the door.
I knew the tenderness that somewhere else
could possibly have been a lover's or a father's
could here be only an efficient way
to minimize the trouble. And yet it seemed
somehow my father was too adept at it,
too skillful, not to feel it in some way.

And feeling it not to need to pull back,
to separate himself from what the rest
of him was doing, which was why, I think,
his face throughout was blank, expressionless,
like the faces of the presidents on the bills
he handed Tony as the door slid shut.
The men fast at the riveters and pressers
and the long row of women at the Singers
were oil now even more than men or women,
mute oil in the loud revving of the place,
a blur of hands on automatic pilot,
slipping the leather through the pumping needles,

under the thrusting rods, the furious hammers,
the nearly invisible whirring of the blades.
"Come on now, Al, it's time," my father said,
and the Captain seemed to grin a little wider,
as if his pleasure there at the end of his

unending day grew freer, more disencumbered,
because he saw me at the start of mine,
under my father's arm, his soft voice broken
against the noise into an unfollowable tune
of favors and petty cash, and how much ass
he had to kiss to get me this, and I
should be a man now and not disappoint him.

The Basement

How many years, decades, since I'd even thought of Gary
when my mother told me on the phone the other night,
in passing, that he'd been thrown in jail for kiting checks,
and that this on top of all the other heartache Gary's mother
had from him, the busted marriage, the drug problems,
had sent her to an early grave. But it wasn't Gary's mother
I thought of as I listened but the basement where we spent
most of our afternoons one summer, the two of us and Helen,
Helen the only German Jew I knew, who'd come after the war
from someplace else, not Germany (though no one told me where),
to live with them, to be his nanny. He called her Zumzing
because she hardly spoke except to ask, every so often,
can I get you zumzing, Gary, you vant zumzing now?
and whether he wanted anything or not he'd answer,
get me zumzing Zumzing, and laugh, so I'd laugh too.
Helen, though, unmindful of the teasing, or inured to it,
which made it easier to do, would hover over Gary,
her readiness to please him unassailable, yet strangely dour,
joyless, like someone on indefinite probation for some crime
nothing she could ever do could quite make up for.

Whenever he'd ask, she'd get the bottle Gary said
wasn't a bottle but a big cigar. Though eight years old,
he'd nuzzle against her, "smoking," gazing at nothing,
Helen stroking his hair, reminding him, Vee don't tell Mama,
dis just our secret, vee don't tell your mama now,

at which he'd pause, grinning, saying Vee dis, vee dat,
with the cigar held gangster style between his fingers.
It never occurred to me to make fun of him.
He'd look up from the bottle from time to time, and smile,
and seem so certain I'd admire him for this, I couldn't not.
It was as if in going down into the basement
he'd gone beyond the reach of how we usually were,
becoming at the same time both older and younger
than he should have been. It thrilled me, being there
with him, all the rules suspended, making new rules up,
the games he'd want to play so like and unlike
the games I knew that to play them was to feel
myself complicit in the secrets he and Helen shared:

Whoever was "it" would be buried under cushions,
and stay there dead while Helen counted to a hundred.
Then "it" would roar and rise and hunt the other down,
whipping him back into the pit where he'd be buried.
Or with the cushions Helen would wall in a corner of the basement,
and Gary and I would take turns guarding each other, marching
back and forth before the entrance, a rifle on one shoulder,
until the prisoner watching for the slightest lapse
would storm the gate, all of the cushions tumbling
down around us as we wrestled to the floor.

I remember reading of the children in the camps and ghettos,
how in their stubborn urge for pleasure where there was no pleasure
they'd pretend the horrors they were living through:
the bigger ones who got to be the Germans whipping and beating
the smaller ones who were the Jews, to dig their graves,
stage funerals, line each other up, and through it all,
German and Jew together, they would all be laughing.
During the war, wouldn't Helen have been about the age
that we were then? I wonder now what she was seeing, or
wanted to see as she looked on, waiting until the play

got too rough, as it always would, and one of us would cry
before she'd pull us off each other and, hugging Gary
or hurrying to get him out another bottle, ask
in the same flat tone, Now vee do zumzing else now, jah?

My mother didn't know where Helen was now,
or whether she went on living with the family
after Gary dropped out of high school and moved away.
She said it drove his mother crazy, how she spoiled him rotten.
Did Helen mourn the trouble he got into? Or had she
by the time we knew her had her fill of mourning,
her heart by then concerned with other things, things he
unwittingly provided, Gary never more enslaved
than in the license she made him think was his? Could he
have been her plaything too, as much as she was his,
her puppet of a secret brooding on what couldn't be forgotten,
all of her life from the war on (and she was just a girl then)
a mere reprise, a deafening echo chamber?
                                                                    And even now
I wonder who's obliging whom when Helen—
after all these years of never being thought of, lost
among the minor people of my personal history—
rises from the dead through small talk to become
my personal link to what I can't imagine.

It almost seems I have my way with her again,
seeing her there in this last scene, down on her knees
surrounded by a chaos of innumerable pieces
of the train set she's saying is like the one she played with
with her papa long ago, an aura of dread and urgency
about her as she hurries to put it all together, working
to keep us down there with her a little longer,
to keep us from going anywhere she wouldn't follow
(did I ever see her leave the house?): all over the basement,
the tracks in curves and straightaways, the signs for Stuttgart,

München, Würzburg, Berlin, the flashing signal lights,
the flagman in the switching yard, black-coated porter at the station,
and beyond it shops, cafés, and houses, a church and school—
the flanged wheels fitted to the tiny rails, and Gary
settled in her lap now, his hands on the black box
easing the levers as she whispers dis one, jah, now dat,
and the cars click forward through that miniature world.
Soon, though, bored, he throws the black box down, and he and I
rampage over everything, stomping and pulling it all apart
while Helen laughs (the only time I ever heard her laugh).

Black Maid

While I'd be wandering through the house you'd just cleaned,
loving the bracing tang of cleanser in the dustless air,
the carpet's thicker shag, the vacuum's streaks and curves
still visible within it, you might have been by then on the bus
to Dudley station, another bus or streetcar taking you
from there to Dorchester, Mattapan, Columbus Street,
or Blue Hill Ave., where you'd have walked the last few blocks
to the once elegant brownstone or triple decker my family
moved away from twenty years before when yours arrived.

Of course I never thought about this then. In my imagination
you were always just Melba, my mother's "girl"; you existed
all through my childhood only once a week, and only here.
All through my childhood, yet how little of you I recall:
the image more a child's drawing of a woman than a woman,
arms and legs too thin for the oval belly, the gray frizzled
pulled-tight bun of hair, the tennis shoes and ankle stockings,
and the image has no voice, and it moves stiffly like a toy,—
no gesture that is yours alone, no word at all between us.

It is as in an underworld I try to make you out,
to recognize you as you might have been, and you,
offended that I'd even want to, or ever think I could
(or for some other reason I cannot conceive),
shrink back into the indistinguishable shadows.
And what I didn't know to ask is only answered now

by the blank gloss of the scrubbed linoleum,
the polished figurines, the made beds smooth as marble:
What was your last name, where did you live?

The Fight

1969

The black girl next to me was cheering under her breath
as the two girls, white and black, appeared to freeze

together for a moment with their hands locked
in each other's hair before they toppled over

in a blur of pummeling. Get the bitch, Dolores,
she was saying, abuse her, eat her up, her faint voice

giddily enraged, yet cautious too, confused,
it almost seemed, uncertain of its own excitement,

as if she'd grown so used to wishing for what she saw
she only half believed she saw it now before her.

Right on, girl, right on, she cheered a little louder,
the voice rousing itself past hesitation or demurral.

And though the rest of us stood there, dumbly looking on,
and would later try hard to range in, cage what we saw

with outrage, stories, rumors of who said what and why,
till we could think it didn't have to do with us,

my friends and I—white friends and black friends—
did any of us at the time make any move to stop it?

Wasn't hers the only voice of what we all were feeling,
and were dismayed to feel, were too well trained to show?

All of us rapt by the tribal solvent of our civil dream,
by the frenzy of slashing nails, ripped blouses, shrieks

and muffled groans; the girls dissolving in the mouth
of rage beyond their names, or sex, or even the history

that carefully prepared them for the dissolution,—
dissolving in the idiot mouth till in the teeth of it

they could only go on tearing at each other, kicking
and scratching even after the teacher intervened.

Cabbie

Only another black kid I didn't need
to notice till he robbed me, and, by then,
of course, knife at my throat, in the unlit street,
it was too late to notice anything.
He, though, when he saw me, what did he see?
Was it dumb luck only that he picked mine out
from so many taxis in that part of town,
that time of night? Or had he studied me?
Through discipline and long experience
alert to what he needed, did he notice
how the fare, the woman and her child
that I was dropping off, were sitting there
beside me, that she and I continued talking
a long time even after she had paid me,
and when she paid me how I took her money
casually, slipping the ten spot into my pocket
with one hand while the other went on gesturing
to whatever story I was telling, as if
the money were a mere formality,
entirely incidental to the friendly talk?
I wonder, too, if he had seen beyond my studied,
even fussily perfected air
of easy feeling, feeling that fell like sunlight
equally on everyone, heedless
of class, position, who was serving whom,
to the desire that the feeling secretly fulfilled,

the mission it accomplished? Did he sense
that it was war I waged, and that the fares
who hailed me down, who saw me only as
another cabbie, were my enemies,
and that my conquest was to entertain,
to interest them in me, in who I was
beyond what I was doing, the tip my tribute,
the size of it, the measure of their defeat?
And did sensing this make me more suitable,
as much a challenge as an easy mark?
making it interesting as well as safe
to lean into the window of the cab
and say his brother had abandoned him,
and he was sick, his ear ached awful, could
I drive him home, he had the money, see,
stuffing the bills down into my pocket
before I even had a chance to answer?

How pleased he must have been, sitting beside me,
as I insisted, his shrewd discrimination
proved by my eagerness to show no fear,
no hesitation when he told me where he lived,
by my wanting him to feel he was a fare
like any other, and to marvel, too,
and like me for the respect I gave,
as if he were a person just as rich
in interest and complexity as I was,
as I drew him out about his family,
his life, and listened, or appeared to listen,
too busy thinking what to ask him next
to even hear what he was saying.
                                    On-coming
traffic flashed like strobe lights through the nearly
total dark within the cab and made
his every move—his head now leaning back

against the seat, and now against the glass,
his hand against his ear, his lips now parted
a little as he moaned—like shuffled stills
of different postures. So I hardly noticed,
or noticed somehow only afterward,
later when he was gone, how all at once,
as in a single gesture, he had cut
the phone cord and was against me with the cool
blade gently, yet more seriously too
for being gentle, tickling my throat,
the wad of bills already in his hand.

He had me get out where there wasn't traffic,
no street light even, at an empty lot.
He had my money. What else did he want?
As if the money were a means to this,
he had me kneel, waving the knife now slowly
before my face, now jabbing at it, not
to cut it, though, just see it flinch, just hear
it beg him not to, don't, please don't. Knife
shearing the world away down to the skin;—
the clever ploys, the camouflage all shredded
like flimsy tissue to the weeping body.
Honky, get your ass out of here, he called,
and I was crawling, searching for the keys
he'd hurled into the lot before he bolted.

And now the knife was simply where I was,
its blade, the broken glass against my hands
and knees, each cut an even sharper opening
of sense, till I was any hunted thing,
just any body on its hands and knees,
helplessly alert, and wholly there.

Pick Up Game

Roxbury 1970

For just a moment whatever history
your life was the wayward arc of crossed with mine.
The only white kid there, I'd come with Dale,
my black friend, to play ball with friends of his.
I'd come because my parents told me not to;
I'd come to prove them wrong, to prove my own
fear wrong and was beginning not to feel it,
my shame of feeling it subsiding now
in the reliable and customary
feints and maneuvers, pump fake, pick and roll,
that made that game like any other game,
letting me think that Dale was just a friend
like any other. Until you appeared—
in high heels, hot pants, flimsy halter neck,
sauntering woozily, more drunk than brazen,
with one hand clutching as if for balance the small
purse slung from your shoulder, while the other hand pointed,
wagging a finger; bemusement and concern
and accusation slurred in your half sung,
white boy, white boy, what you doin' here?

Though I pretended not to see or hear you,
and in a moment you were gone, forgotten,
never to be thought of once in all
these years, just as I'd hardly think of Dale   /
once I had graduated and gone on
to where you knew I all along was going,
your voice returns now like a prophesy
aimed and propelled, it seems, by everything
that brought us from our separate origins
to that chance meeting and then through it toward
our separate destinations, which for you
and Dale was probably where you were already,
and for me, another suburb like the one
I had to hide from for our lives to cross.
Your voice returns, resounds with what it was
my privilege to forget—that it, too, was just
another game, my being there with Dale,
our being friends, a game that I played through
him with my parents, not to prove them wrong,
but just to worry them, the bold transgressor,
rebelling carefully where it didn't matter,
and dutifully conforming where it did.

White boy, white boy, what you doin' here?
What you doin'? over and over now
you call more clearly as I turn away,
as Dale drives, spins into the lane and rises
as if against the gravity your voice
articulates—what did I know about him?
what did I want to know beyond the hunger,
and the beauty in the hunger, of the taut,
gleam-chiseled body that could never quite
rise high enough above the rim, or hang there
long enough, or soft enough float down?

Between Assassinations

Old court. Old chain net hanging in frayed links from the rim,
the metal backboard dented, darker where the ball
for over thirty years has kissed it, the blacktop buckling,
the white lines nearly worn away. Old common ground
where none of the black men warming up before the basket
will answer or even look in my direction when I ask
if I can run too, the chill a mutual understanding,
one of the last we share, letting me join them here,
if nowhere else, by not letting me forget I don't belong.

Old court. Old courtesy, handshake, exchange of names,
in the early days of bussing, between assassinations,
before our quaint welcoming of them had come to seem,
even to ourselves, the haughty overflow of wealth
so thoroughly our own we didn't need to see it.
Old beautiful delusion in those courtly gestures
that everything now beyond our wanting just to play
was out of bounds, and we were free between the white lines
of whatever we assumed we each of us assumed.

Old court, old dream dreamed by the weave, the trap,
the backdoor pass. Old fluid legacy, among the others,
that conjures even now within our bodies and between them
such a useless, such an intimate forgetting, as in the moment
when you get a step on your defender and can tell
exactly by how another man comes at you

where your own man is and, without looking, lob the ball
up in the air so perfectly as he arrives that
in a single motion he can catch and finger roll it in.

Old court. Old dwindling cease fire, with no hope of peace,
that we silently turn away from when the game is over,
hurrying back (as if believing contact meant contagion)
to our separate tribes, to the cleansing fires of what,
despite ourselves, we momentarily forgot:
old lore, old news, old burning certitudes we can't
stoke high or hot enough, yet won't stop ever stoking
until whatever it is we think we are anneals
and toughens into an impenetrable shield.